Ghost
Sickness

Ghost Sickness

LUIS ALBERTO URREA

Cinco Puntos Press
El Paso, Texas

FIRST EDITION

Library of Congress Cataloging-in-Publication Data

    Urrea, Luis Alberto.
      Ghost sickness : a book of poems / by Luis Alberto Urrea.
          p.   cm.
      ISBN 0-938317-30-X (paper)
        1. Mexican-American Border Region—Poetry. 2. Family—Mexico-Tijuana (Baja California)—Poetry. 3. Mexican Americans—Poetry.
      I. Title.
      PS3571.R74G47 1997
      811'.54—dc21
                                       97-20643
                                          CIP

Cover photo. "Marilyn in Ciudad Juárez" Copyright © 1996 by Virgil Hancock. This photograph and others that explore contemporary urban Chihuahua, Mexico appear in his book of photographs, *Chihuahua, Pictures from the Edge*, published by University of New Mexico Press. Cinco Puntos Press would like to thank Virgil for his continuing support.

Cover and book design by Vicki Trego Hill of El Paso, Texas.

Contents

NOTES & ACKNOWLEDGEMENTS

Ghost Sickness has mutated over the years into several books, through myriad revisions and excisions and additions. Portions of this book have first been published in the following anthologies: *The Best American Poetry, 1996*: thank you, Adrienne Rich and David Lehman; *Edges*: thank you, Ursula K. Le Guin and Virginia Kidd.

Other poems and fragments of poems have appeared in the following journals: *Maize*: thank you, Alurista; *Many Mountains Moving*: thank you, Naomi Horii and Marilyn Krysl; *Puerto del Sol*: thank you, Vickie Lloyd; *Sniper Logic*: thank you, Karen Auvinen.

Readers and editors have offered suggestions on this manuscript for several years. Donald Wesling and César A. González witnessed my first attempts. Diane Wakoski gave me kind words and thoughtful feedback in the 1980's. Ese canijo del Ben Sáenz gave me a tough and needed reading in the 1990's. Parts of "Ghost Sickness" have been refined through readings and talks all over the country. All the listeners and co-readers who responded to the work helped to shape it.

And Bobby and Lee and Susie Byrd have brought it all to life.

Finally: thank you always to my Cinderella, y Viva Teresita Urrea—la Santa de Cabora.

This one's for my soul's sister,
Esperanza Urrea.

PART ONE

Ghost Sickness

Ghost Sickness

this is the sound of poisons
the sickness no one knows

                              shriekback

I.

I saw the dead nodding sugar skulls.
They danced dark alleys bright
from burning.
Children licked the letters of their names
from glassy candy foreheads. Whorehouse poets
whispered sly reports
to ice cream suited gunmen.

Did you see the federales fall,
spin beneath dry aqueducts and drop,
machine-gunned by four hungry ghosts,
adobe coats punched red in blooded blossoms?

In blackest deserts Pancho Villa headless
sank to hollow knees
to plead with countless sleeping graveyard bones
to take him home, to find the road he could not see,
to fill his empty hands with dreaming.

Antlers of smoke from maquiladoras rising.
Bluecoat children with radium blood
stood at day-long counters hard-
wiring RCA, IBM, ITT, ICBM: 10 cents
an hour: red flowers already in their wombs,

they fought for room at taco stands, the whistle blew
and they flowed, the blue tide of Tijuana,
Tecate, Mexicali, Matamoros. Fat
sputtered and spattered on fuming coals. Old
men drowsed on filth-shined curbs. Sienna cheeks
carved into riverruns of wrinkle: relief
maps of forget.
We followed the Mexican road,
rolled all that dark feathered snake-spine
that looped doomed volcanoes. The sad
sore-backed trucks
hauled tall dust-frosted loads
      lava grit fans
      thrown free
      on loose turns

      would flee
      down the slopes:
            fistfuls of stony whispers.

My dead father at the wheel.
One cool hand on the gears, one gray arm
out the window, cocked: cigarette aimed at the sun,
firing sparks, white whorls
on his smoky muscles
      gone soft in the wind,
          in the grave, loose—
            ripped
                  in the wind—
                    he flinched

and the houses
on highway's edge
flashed past,
so many
scattered post-cards—
feverlight
in every door:
grandfathers leaned canes against benches,
women combed rivers from their heads,
parrots flaming in cages.
My father said
            There's nothing left.

Children at roadside
shot wooden rifles:
paz-paz-paz: sold armadillos
in small paper boxes: danced
at the brink of barrancas:
lived
13 yards   ,
from the roadside.

We dug as we sped
an unbreachable trench
full of longing,
shadows,
radio music.

2.

I fled this land with The Man.
Northern borders rolled off my barbed-wire back.
My shadow, shredded as a wetback's shirt
still flapping.

How could I become
who I would be: I searched for the future me
in the eyes of men, some signal,
some sign: so mad was I
for manhood.

To be
          a cowboy.
To be
          a big daddy.
To be
          el mero chingón de estos rumbos
          y si no les gusta, les echo la tierra encima.
To be
          a lover of women.
To be
          a jimihendrix.
To be
          anything but what I was.

What made these men return
each night, dreams dented,
worries tightening as they climbed the steps:
Kiss the wife Set the clock 6 a.m. Pay the gas
Warm the car Shovel snow No sit-ups tonight

Heart attack Cholesterol Pay the rent Lunch box
Cold coffee no sugar little cream
Daughter's puberty Athlete's foot Overtime Fill er up
Dan Rather Graveyard shift Iran Iraq Crack Beer
IRS GMC CBS HUD PMS BVD Bald headed Bad breath
Bad back Bad luck Bad check
and boyhopes
folded under flightless wings.

Did Mexicans trudge home
through bad dream streetlights? My father did.
Until he did
not.

3.

He didn't come back.
He with his manhood smells
I tracked all those miles:
his tobacco smell,
his machinery smell,
his playboy coffee break smell.
His foot powder
his sorrowful
his hungry
angry
lonely
tired
armpit, hair tonic
father's smell.

From the grave to the womb
he fled.

His eyes pure as mirrors
told me
nothing.

4.

Drought killed the cattle. The sun's hard fist
milked them dry, dropped them
in pools of their own shadow.

Waterless.

On highway shoulder, cows
upturned: 4 legs stiff
as furniture. Upholstery gutted
by obsidian vultures: sofas of death
tumbled,
dismantled.

Such heat.

Our lips white paper.
Red calligraphy of laughter.
Such heat
on the land where night
grows thin callouses of snow
on high plateaus gone clear by dawn
to steam.

The road
left a perfect impression of me
cut out every micro-
millimeter of wind,
the moon
rolled thick as an eye
sunburned white.

5.

Down the coast
turtle hunters lay
in seaside shacks
trapped
in wrapping nets
of heat.
Women
bundled in sand
dark breathing
knots of shade.
Dry turtle shells
rocked
in wind,
tocked
like ancient clocks.

The hunters twitched
caught
in dreams
of waves

sunfish
blood.
Hungry men
burned black.
Men who smell sealanes
even in sleep.

—for James Atlee Phillips

6.

Alive, he dreamed loud.
He slept in sleeveless undershirts, white pubic hair
a heart-shaped ghost. Two groaning beds, neon windows, fans
chewed flies to slivers, spit
them over us: thin rain
of legs, antennae.

Geckos on the walls
licked spiders from the brick.

And then his dreaming.

He ground his teeth and spun,
a dense pale star
tied in sheets: his teeth
chipped off, they cheeped
trapped in his mouth.
I cringed.
I longed to reach him, slap him
in his sleep, in hotel rooms, at midnight, one

o'clock, two o'clock, three: stretch across that wailing
wall of grief, cry
        stop it, wake up. Halt
the grinding shatter of his chewing.

What cold dream drove him across the bed?
What infection of the soul took hold of his mouth?
Did his raw stumps strike sparks? Ignite
the scattered leaves of unsaid words across his tongue?

My hand hung frozen over him.
All the cities feared the metal scream
of my one father swallowing his teeth.

7.

Crazy for the Go-Go's, crazy
in love with anything
on the radio,
he speeds:

rivers wear long wigs of fog,
the road full of snakes
coiling first timid throbs of heat,
buzzards swim the centerline
six foot shadows wobbly
as fish underwater.

Semis bomb the car,
their bow-waves shake him like sobs, and he's hollowing the
distance, carving the hills
off the horizon:

the small hard nuggets of her scent
burn in his hands.

He has driven this road before.
He asks at every station for a map.
No one speaks his language anymore.

Speed is prayer.
It's all he can muster.
His layers peel back
the faster he goes,
his memories curl off him,
tug the hems of nightmares: snap
away in hurtling wind:
       & he thinks
       if you just go fast enough,
your sins might fall before your fuel
is gone. Your shadow, winded,
might drop.
       If you just go fast enough,
time might stop
ticking you off.

8.

It was three a.m., at least that late. The
bus terminal was on a long unlit highway. It
was so hot, your back slid across the seat on
a cushion of grease. And the water was just
poison. We pulled in for a Coke, to wash the
tiny dust clods down our throats. The roof

was made of vapor lights; it flickered,
flickered; moths the size of doves battered
up against the tubes. 2 Americans stood at
the window, haggling over bus fare. Half of
the place was a diner, darkened, on the far
side of the room. A few tables, really,
three stools at a counter. I stood staring.
A kid sat at the table, in the shadows,
grunting. He was lost in rolls of fat. Fat
hung over the back of his t-shirt collar from
his neck. His eyes were the size of beans,
pushed deep in the slack yellow bulges of his
face. I could hear his mouth work, these
little wet sounds. He poured sugar into his
fist from one of those table-top sugar
dispensers with the slanted chrome top. You
know them? He was pouring sugar into his
fist like his fist was a coffee cup, filling
his fist then tipping back his head—the lard
welled up in a flat disk, the rings of Saturn
clogging his pulse—and he poured the sugar
in. Were those 2 at the counter his? Were
they parents? With their backs turned,
hunched against his grunts, his tiny eyes
locked on my face, his small wet clicks. He
licked the gravel off his lips. Stared.
Stared at me. Little noises. Grunting.
Pouring, pouring, swallowing, fist after
fist, all night, abandoned.

Hello I said to him.
Brother!

9.

My father pale as a fingernail
drives demonic
across ghost-heavy night.

10.

So you're a man, he said. *How much life does it take
to be a man,* he said. *How much life?*

On a river bank

       tired

  women bent to meet their shadows.

     Stones
      pale as Easter eggs
    staggered.

Someone laughed.

Sheets
    blew
       wide
         as flags
           in unexpected
      wind!

Back-
lit,
legs.

X-rayed.
Wide:
      arms held high:

              flight

                  on earth:

                    ecstatic

mundane.

Shirts, skirts, undershirts.
Diapers, bras, secret
      colored
      women
      things,

      thrown in
      scrubbed
      pounded:

      foam
            launched
      itself:

      bubble tugboats, icebergs, dragons
      went down
      through the village.

One radio crackled: Love
in cities never seen:
Canta y no llores, porque cantando
se alegran
            Cielito Lindo
los corazones!

                    All that black hair
                    straight
                    down
                    their backs
        over shoulders

                    writing
                    in
                            tri
                                cate
stanzas across their necks. Bare legs bruised purple. Burned
summer dark. Sweat

strung from throats to collarbones clear priceless beads
                            broke
their strings and hit
water

etched a codex

                        I daily
                        try

                    to decipher.

II.

Nayarit.

Emerald atmosphere
hung between green volcanoes
smoked dark to cover skies
as hard as domes.

Starved men in white
vivid from the road
as ibis
picked
along cucumber rows.

Trucks,
rattle-backed,
humped the harvest
untasted
upslope, out
of the field, up
to the highway, away
to Mazatlán,
Hermosillo,
Guaymas: to trains:
to transport ships: to salads
in Orange County.

One truck
in a slick of cucumber mush
spun, slipped
sideways, hit
the berm
and flipped.

Explosion
of cucumber shrapnel:
pepinos rocketed
in every direction:
 ¡cataplum!

Pickled in Pemex.

Driver climbed out, spit,
said *Chingue a su madre,*
and marched into the pickle field,
fuming.

Flocking,
fast, like a feathery wind,
they came.
From fields
two farms away,
circling in.

Thin-backed, long-necked, flapping.
Swoop. Swoop and clutch. Swoop
and speed to the shade of trees.
Food, man, food
everywhere.

Their rush,
their call:
they were bright in the sun
smoking cigarettes
spitting seeds
as the laughter of birds.

12.

Hit it.

Drive mad across town, radio tuned
to sizzle-spit mariachi howls, drunken wide-hat wolves,
sixgun poets bawling pagan gospel of tequila

love
murder
ruin.
Six men in a Volkswagen, uncountable ghosts on the roof
       hung on for dear death, rubber burn on cobbles
       as we spun another corner, laughter's nasty
       calliope calling, dogbark
       midnight outskirts
of some flyspeck town,
cemetery next door
to the whorehouse, away
where the shouts and the shooting
and the trumpets and the shatter wake no one.
Grass shacks lined the compound where the women slept
with washtubs, tv's, candy, photos, vinegar,
cigarettes, magazines, radios, memories, dreams,
chamber pots, underpants, razor blades, make-up,
bottles, babies, nightmares, and one bundle each
of rubber-band letters from some dreamboy who went
and never came home.

Dig the sign: CLUB VERDE PARA HOMBRES:
       CUELGEN SUS PISTOLAS.
Hang up your pistols, boys. Fat cops at the door
touched us all over, felt us for hardness under our clothes,
pulled from men's belts .38s, .44s, hung them
on pegs by the bar. Dark stench of toilets
let run from the stalls. Drunks kneeling
at the bowls, penitent supplicants
to the Virgin of Filth. And inside—
shaky-legged tables

of tin—flaking stickers stuck
to our forearms, bright
paper freckles: TECATE
DOS EQUIS
CORONA
CARTA
BLANCA.

Homosexual bartender's long blue eyelids.

     Concrete dance floor stained
into maps of lost worlds
by spilled beer, by bootheels, by flat
women's sandals.
Black hair dyed orange
as cheap boots.
Black armpit feathers plastered with sweat.
In that corner, rock and roll:
the blind guitarist
followed the sounds
with his head, thin as sticks,
sang:

Old jou need es lob.

Love is all you need.
Love is all you need.
You can buy it here.
Unzip your hair, pull off your skin.
We watched them dance—farmhands
worked hard at having fun, the whores
     raised crops from them and pulled them
     off to harvest.

All those dresses
in the farmers' hands gone limp
wilted
by 1,000 palms.
We danced with them.
Love is all you need.

Around the room
cheap wooden doors
let light escape
in yellow stripes
from closetrooms
with 1 bed each,1
light. 1 jug. 1 bowl.
1 woman.
1 filmy
sexy girlie thing
flung over the 1
wooden chair.
No exit.

I saw the crucifix above the bed, then her.

Cigarette burns tattooed her skinny arms.
Through an open door
I saw.
Love is all you need.
She dipped a knotted flower
rag into her bowl, ran water down her chest, her neck, her leg,
       then opening her thighs her other leg
        so tired it shook. I knew
that hair as thin as mist

uncurled from moistened flesh and rose.
She wiped her nodding breasts under her dress, washed off
        the heat,
washed off the weight from her brown ribs, washed off
        the smell, the feel, the
fingerprints.

And then looked up.

I smiled across the room, embarrassed rogue
through sheets of smoke.
Her stare burned my smile to ash.

You smile so easily, muchacho.
You think you offer me
condolences, or is this
business? Do you
think you understand?

        Love is all you need.

You'll never understand
until you lie here
ten or twenty nights
and think of home.

        Love is all you need.

You can spend money
to rest in me.
I'll carry you.
Would you carry me?
And if we meet at noon

        Love is all you need.

in the town plazuela,
you with your notebooks
and me with my flowers
always careful not to greet
anybody

Love is all you need.

you will look away.
Ashamed at what you put here.
And I will walk away
out of town the long way
because the finest part of me you bought
was silence.

Love is all you need.

Neither one looks back.
Then you go
but I remain
tomorrow
and tomorrow
and tomorrow.

Love is all you need.
Her lips were smeared, the color of crushed smiles.
I pointed to my mouth. She wiped her face. The knot
of cotton flowers cleaned her teeth.
We waved.

The blind guitarist shrieking in the corner.
The twisted Jesus writhing in His torture.
The brilliant coin cascade that hit her bed, a dark ranchero
         pushing in, she glanced at me, her hands

at forehead, heart: sign of the cross. The closing door.
She loves you yeah, yeah, yeah.

13.

and he drives

I watch him

he drives

all fields burn black around him

his engine coughing sparks

fire skips

empty rivers

mummies twitch underground

he's laughing

I watch him

his engine coughing blood

flaming ravens hit the windshield

all those feathers

and he drives

and I watch.

14.

Mi padre, muerto
ya por interminables años, no me deja
en paz: no se quiere ir: lo veo
cada día. Mi viejo se esconde
en los árboles, en el agua, en
las nubes de humo que huyen
de los cigarros de secretarias. O se mete
como ladrón
por mis ventanas
y me roba la comida. Es vivo: es capaz
de esconderse en la luna.
Y me dice,
      —Hijo, no queda nada.
        No queda nada.

Mi padre, sembrado
en su tierra Mejicana, echando retoños
en la pradera obscura del olvido, brilla:
cuando apago la luz, su cara
tira chispas en la esquina. Cuando
hago el amor, viene
corriendo. Cuando salgo
a la calle, me persigue
por los ojos
de niños callejeros.
Usa tacones de oro.
Me huele el café.
Lo veo
sin verlo.

25

Y me dice,

      —Hijo, no queda nada.
     No queda nada.

Mi padre, muerto ya y hecho polvo, llora
lagrimas de barro. Con voz de piedra me grita, me canta
su último consejo:
      —Hijo, tu vida es una moneda.
     Gástate bien. Porque
     no queda nada.
     No queda nada de mí.

15.

Now I know
what you tried to tell me:

the wind eats coyotes.

It'll swallow us too
who stand still long enough.
Even ore trains dense as stars
tumble in the desert wind:
engines flat-faced as vipers
disappear.

The wind eats the hills,
fossils fall to talc.

The far horizon folds up:
tumbleweeds carry off
our Mexico:

ten thousand miles of breath
collects beneath the moon,
coughs out our used-up names,
and stirs.

We can't escape the blow:
our prison bars
are memories,
are bones.

PART TWO

Divorce
and other Incidents

Wetback's National Anthem

we feed
you you
bastards
the least
you could
do is
listen

The Garbage-Picker Speaks

—Tijuana Municipal Garbage Dump

Look sharp.
Trucks pull down the mountain of glass.
You could be buried in windows
open on a sky
of feathers.
Trash flash-floods,
storming gulls,
a fog of cries.
I pulled open her dress
on a mattress full of smoke,
I took her wooden nipples
into my desert mouth
and I sucked until dreams
dripped out of her like beads.
She gives me 2 tortillas
and a pinch of salt.
I squeeze 3 drops of lime
and think I'm tasting her.

I wrap the strap around my head
day's end
and climb the slope, my sack
of bottles, tin, bones.
Above us, graves
sprout crossed wood blossoms—
calm garden of grief
between the trash and home
where my daughter plays

with uncertain ghosts
who can't get back
to Oaxaca.

Late tonight, at the hole,
I wipe myself with leaves.

What we find, we sell
to buy one night of sleep.
Then tractors
bid us rise.
Take up our staffs, go back
attack what is forgotten.
Day-long every day
we sip at the shore of ourselves,
we drink an elixir of sweat,
we are pools that never dry.

We only own our eyes.

La cara perdida

Es invierno
y te escribo a través
de este silencio largo.
Si pudieras ver lo que he dejado
bajo el cielito negro
de este llano. Tres poemas
amargas. Mil figurinas
de plomo. Mi nombre.
Fotografías
de un vestido
azul. Y
tu cara.

Soy un hombre sincero
de donde mueren las palmas.
Mi infancia fue
un jardín de fuego.
Y tú, ¿qué supiste
de mí?
Antes de tocarte la cara,
la perdí.

—Carmen

To A Black Child in the Rain

1-24-90: Boston

Only when he has a family
does a man learn
true loneliness.

I saw you
wait
a line of white-faced cars
impatient
to cut down
filter roads
to work.

It took me this long
to arrive
at our shared morning—
to leave home before light,
paper sack soaking through
with sandwiches, pretzels,
an apple. V-8 for me,
how about you? Juice?

Just wait
until you leave your wife
asleep in your warm bed.
The engine heats itself
on a dark and empty street.
Morning deejay pretends
that he's your friend.

And the comforting
lonesome slap
of the windshield wipers
leads you
through the stalled-out
morning rush
of other men
choked to death by
neckties
paychecks
worry
rain.

You stood alone,
rubber boots in slushy pools.
I stopped
the traffic: we lined up
and watched you skip
across the road, so cold.
I watched you go,
unknowing.

You and me, kid.
Early morning.
Growing up.

The First Lowrider in Heaven

I am thinking of the vato I went to see in his coffin.

He was ugly, flaco, tattooed, long-haired, laid-out.

He had on a suit.

Looked pissed off.

No, he looked sad.

And pissed off.

The way vatos look right before they kick your ass.

Muy chucote, el buey.

Y bien jodido, too, porque he was bien dead.

So his ass was already kicked.

I looked in on him—he smelled like medicine and cotton.

I didn't even know him.

I was there for political support.

Homeboys sniffling, tears filling their blue teardrop tattoos.

Rucas dressed in wedding, baptism, quinceañera dresses.

And the dead guy lying there, sharp in his suit.

Snug in silver-white satin.

Shot himself in the head.

Old women, cowboy-booted fathers, crying over him.

No telling now, in his boxed sainthood, if he smoked crack,
  gang-banged, carried shivs, hit his mother, kicked
  the dog.

Death had purified him.

He was now an angel.

Low-riding the clouds.

Put the gun in his mouth.

His lover, you know.

Told him her love for him had turned to smoke.

They went to a movie first, y la loca sent him away. Forever.

He walked in circles.

He had no words for the poems he needed to send.

He could only say, *What's the pedo, homeys?*

There were no words.

So he kissed the round hole of the .44.

Right where her kisses had gone.

Put it where her tongue flicked spit off his.

Pinche love, ese, they were saying.

A magnum, just like Dirty Harry: tear a hole through an
  engine block, vato—I heard them whispering.

Taste of gun oil where her bubblegum breath had blown.

Her insistent flavor of smoke, salt, lemon.

He had her panties in a drawer, pobrecito.

He had her letter in his pocket.

I looked at his eyes; boy, they sure were dry now.

Then I noticed the pillow.

No indentation.

Smooth silver satin.

All shiny and curved.

His head went as far as his ears.

Beyond that, feathers.

That ruca he loved was in flight.

She took with her the odors of her body.

She took the funny loops of her writing.

She took the Easter menudo breakfast with her papi.

She took their favorite television show—he went from channel
to channel, couldn't find it anywhere.

She took the lipstick, the Secret roll-on, the Tic-Tacs, the way
she cried out when she came, the way she said his name when
she awoke, the sea coast of her hair, the swoop of her
belly, the babymouth of her navel, the beautiful lies she
believed and whispered in his ear—words like familia,
always, soul-mates.

He liked that soul-mates onda.

She took off through the engine block of his dreams.

His mind held tight in her fingers.

Flavor of steel and powder.

Smoke rings followed her.

Aloft.

Across the Street

My mother died. My wife and I
drove across the country, then down
5000 miles in a Subaru
to her house.
I couldn't sleep, convinced
my mother's coughing ghost
would be revealed in the kitchen
brewing coffee, squinting
to see if that shadow on the back lawn
was a bird or a rock.
I'd get up & water the front.
The guy across the street had gone someplace dark
years ago. Now he was back, making a go of it
with his parents. All of them in a sterile house
sipping bourbon, eating foil-wrapped tv dinners.
Each day he studiously blew three hours' worth
of harmonica, wheedling his way through
folk albums from the 60's. Utterly
off.

Came over one day and said: "Do you
        talk
to my father?
—I'm schizophrenic.
        Did you
                    know
that?
Gone more than a year.

Fucking dirt!
    I hate that…fucking

                dirt! Put down that clod!
I loved your mother. God
    damn it.
        Hold me.
           Hold me.
             Praise God.
                Praise the Lord.   I'm a born-again
Christian.
I was in a hospital.
Hold me.
      Hold me.
         Hold me.
         Now!"

They took him away.
He's been gone a long time. But
now his old man shuffles over every day,
crossing the black street,
says: "When you gonna do something
    about that lawn?"
He asks in the morning, then about a half hour later:
    "Hey man,
when you gonna do something
      about that lawn? It's
uh
    looking yellow. I say
hey, man,
when
you

gonna
do
something
         you know
about
that lawn?"

His Mrs. hides inside.
I hear him asking
my wife, my friends, the neighbors
two, three times a day.
       "Hey man," he says
like the idea just came to him, his eyes bleak
as chips of ice, orange
tobacco tanning his fingertips
and one fourth
of his mustache
accidentally
sliced off,
       "when you gonna do
something…"
looking at the dirt
like he's discovered a secret
       "…about that lawn?"

He drives his car
into the side of a truck.
Peels half the fender
right off, then
lights a cigarette and shuffles home, car dripping
on the corner. His Mrs. says, "Oh
Tom!"

I catch him
holding my hose, peering
in the window to see
if my wife's running
around in her underpants,
dirt on his cuffs.
And he says,
     "When my boy
comes home,
     I think we're gonna
do something
     about you
and that stinkin lawn."

But his boy is never coming back.
And California crumbles
like dust.

N.

Sought peace
on fractured pan of flash-flood
desert lowlands: had a woman's name
on my tongue, it started with the letter N: the
rest of her name evaporated. Air was
so blue you could split it with a kick: it'd crack
in china chips. Far enough away from the road
so shouts fell dull in dusty silence, I knelt.
Felt the whole thing grind into gear—the USA hit
second and I'm not kidding, burned rubber
across the earth, carrying N
in the back seat. The earth
peeled out across the stars, the stars
drove down an ant hole, I
stood there with my hat
on backwards.

The ground crumbled.
Snake eggs lay around me, burst.
Brown. Wind-husked as dried orange skins.
Honda tracks slit the sand,
flattened finger-slender
baby snakes. They lay
knotted as
leather ribbons.
Who's to blame?

The snakes saw light, hoped.
Came forth. I know
about coming in hope.
I once
saw N. But the snakes,
had they lived,
would have eagerly sunk
their needle-bright teeth in me, and end
of story. Or

they would have bit
clean-furred field mouse
who
seeing light
were hoping for a seed
in the hopeful grip
of a beetle who
also hoped for a miraculous
dung ball.

But, hung across the handlebars,
he came:
dreaming of his girl, hell
he was probably dreaming about N: everybody else
was. But, hung across the handlebars,
he came hoping
for one last bitchen ride
before he had to load the bike
onto dad's trailer, wheel home, mow
the lawn, do his math, remedial
summer school reading: he came
farting over the dune,

side-slipped and smeared
the hope of these sidewinders:
unraveled them beneath their light
which suddenly turned harsh: baked
their fabric dry: took their eyes: tightened them
into jerky for the star-struck ants.
I know about this unraveling.

Well, quiet settled in:
ants carried off strips of skin:
bones sprawled rosy, ribs
splayed like timbers
from the big shipwreck: watery
shadows in the wheel rut sand.
As I walked away, a Spanish Bayonet
lanced my leg, sprayed
delicious blood over the tongue
of the desert.
There was no one else to drink it.
I wasn't in love anymore.
And besides,
all the sharks were gone.
Dead and burned to powder, oil.
They're in the engines of the Hondas now.
Killing everything.

—*Nicolina*

Driving Away

This is the end
behind the ending.

◆

After your marriage
you marry a highway.

◆

After the highway
you marry your shadow.

◆

Licking his shadow
the driver falls on snowbanks—
fills his mouth with crows.

◆

High Plains frozen hard
as a plate.

Joe Ely tucked in the speakers
in the door.

Black cowboy hat &
a white waitress.

I eat my shadow at the
Last Chance Cafe.

◆

There are 100 different kinds
of divorce.

◆

And I cannot be found.

◆

She
wears
cloaks
of webs,
spiders
dense
as pearls
at her heart,
hangs
dew
at
her ankles
small stones
of water,
between
her legs
a photograph
of
birthdays.

she speaks
in a rustle
of wind

through
prairie,
sings:
small
bones,
blue
feather,
wings,
fossil…
or so
she says
but these
days
I can't
hear
her.

◆

They looked for me, afterwards.

I was scraps, tatters

hung from raven's beak.

They say

the strips of me

were arrayed

in the initials

of your name.

◆

This is the way the world ends: Angels
Harley down Sierra arroyos
Blueskin oilsmoke
Peels off the road. Horses
Beneath them scream
Hard-throated as
Wasps.

       The body in the sand sifts to dust,
       Tans to leather.

You drive the Front Range in a pickup,
Your lover cuts salami from a log, lifts
Meat disks to his tongue on the ice
Of a folding buck blade. His eyes
Rich with your body, flick
The horizon, scan
For elk.

       Dead men board the A train
       In Manahatta's bloodrust tunnels.

He can smell you
on his collar.

◆

The contrails will remind me of vast thumbnails
scraping pigment from the sky. I will stand in a blue
pool of shadow, watch the bombers drift over the
Chocolate Mountains. The desert will be cold, the air
will be bright with the storm of my breathing. Each
breath will taste like sugar.

I will speed for 7 days, half watching for you in the mirrors.
The world will be filled with rattling trucks: in every
landscape, a Chevy. All radios blaring the news. All the
Mexicans in the country will be heading back for any
border, waving   *bye-bye,*

amigos.
>   *Bye-*

>   *bye.*

♦

Far from me,
the Day enters your window as you drive.
You were always impatient: now, it's here.
In its grip, your throat
throbs with lost songs
whispers melt behind your lips,
what you meant to say to me
dense upon your tongue
as jade.
>   Your life the slightest deer
>   Stumbling before the dogs.

♦

Had a wife, the raven said.

She swallowed parts of me
like inky poems, sardines.
I parted her feathers
to look at the pink
of her belly.

Had a wife
who said
*I'm ashamed to be seen in public
with you.*

The hunters shook their heads.
Here, they said. *Let us help you.*
Put a bullet through his eyes.

Had a lover, the raven said,
feeling along the ground
for food.

The hunters shook their heads,
said *Some shadows won't even
learn from the sun.*
Walked off smoking
Cuban cigars.

Raven could only find ashes,
poisoned ashes
to eat.

◆

I found a poem on I-25, fleeing the ruins of my marriage,
heading south at 85 mph. I was into New Mexico, on my
way to further disasters.

The ground everywhere was frozen—for 50 miles in any
direction a man could have found nowhere to stand.
The roadsign is still frozen.

It sings:

> Eagles Nest
> Red River
> Angel Fire

◆

Tom Horn's Letter to Charley Irwin
from the Cheyenne Jail—March 5, 1903:

This

winter

does

look

to me

like

a

corker.

The

back

bone

of

it

may

soon

break.

◆

We stare at new atrocities now.

◆

El sexo. Laberinto de sombras. Aguardiente. Olas rojas, venas, nubes. Hicieron el amor: las hojas caeron, en el viento cabalgaban, el sonido igual a la canción de tus uñas razuñando al piso. Espuma. Y allí, a tus lados, firmaste tu nombre…sangre sobre la madera. El sexo. Es solamente un sueño, y despues, no te acuerdas de las caras.

◆

Sitting at Tom Horn's grave. Me & all the other dead men taking our afternoon leisure. My wife behind in her suffering, weeping on the porch. The agony of a wife. So I sit by the grave of the "exterminator." His rosy headstone reads: "IN LOVING MEMORY OF TOM HORN 1861-1903." You see, somebody loved the killer, even after he himself was killed.

Nearby, in this boneyard, someone plucks a banjo. It's weird, a sound Tom himself would recognize, some settler's ghost working through the scales with the tireless 19th-century banjo sound. Tom Horn's toebones slowly beginning to tap. He's smiling. The dead are always happy — just look at how their skulls keep grinning.

Tom Horn knew how to kill; if only I could learn how to live.

◆

My God! we cry. Look
at those special effects, will you.

Our feet stick to the floor.

We hang like cutouts and gawk.

On the screen, we star
in a movie known in

this country's translation

as:

Spontaneous Human Combustion.

◆

The ghosts of our ancestors
man the morals committee:

all love scenes
snipped.

◆

It's only this endless distress.

◆

Seen From a Boston Bus in Mid Winter:
a lone man
broke
through Charles River ice—

clenched his arms
to himself,
dropped through thick water
trailing memories like bubbles:
her face,
    her laughter,
               her
                    strangely bumpy
                              nipples,
her—
      self.

I stood at the window
with black men, all
of us blowing
steam into our fists
as firemen
tried to untangle
lifelines, &
the man
beside me

launched steam words against
the uncaring glass,
spoke what I remember now
staring at myself
as I sink in summer's
moronic light,
exhausted sparrows
of my hope stretched out
sleeping in the street:

*If you ain't goin' to break through the ice,
then walk on it.*

*If you goin' to break through the ice,
stay—the fuck—off!*

I said

Do I know you?

◆

Tonight: how stupid
can you get: you phone

your lost woman to hear
her answering machine: it no
longer mentions you: & to make things
worse, you don't even stop at doing it
once.

◆

What have they done to the day?
Buried it in creeping shade.
Lizard clouds above L.A.
Where the mystery is laid.
I watched the lightning
As it played
Across the rooftops....
Sweetheart, is it safe?

Women hang laundry up there
Smoke is the skirt at their legs
Raindrops like beads in their hair
And light sinks into its dregs.
I watched the lightning
As it played
Across the rooftops.
Darling, is it late?

◆

I turn from child to dust
before dusk's curtains fall
unfelt across the Sierra

the gravel of my life
drops from the treads of God's dark boots
and like stars or suns that gleam
in the passion of a sudden flare-up,
I spin away

down unknown maelstroms
across immense empty spaces
in vast untouched chambers

one   one   one

                        alone   (forever)

Dntn.

It's
rush hr
some
where
else

&

out on
5th
a
girl
-child
in white
dress

braces

holds
1
gold
Twinkie
w/ 2
fingers
bites

licks
the cream

w/ the
tip
of her tongue

watches

1 bloated
jet
barely make it
out
of the sky

hard
hats
rise
from
holes

watch

her watch
the plane
& 1
fat man
w/ 1
arm

bumps

into her
looks

like he's
going
to cry

watch

ing
them
watch
her
watch

ing
those
others

drop

out of
sky dreams
out of
jet
streams
out of
there
& in
to here

while
bus
drivers

blow
in
discrete
smoke
all over her
legs

in
side
the
tobacco
shop
in
the
pen
sioners
ho
tel
time
drools
down
the
chin
of
the day

&

pen
sioners
shop

for
to
bacco
think

ing
why
my pappy
back in
ought
nine or
was
it
ten
called
his Red
Man
in
pouches
'baccy'

pause

thin
stained
men
turn
away

from her
hair

her tongue
her legs
remember
sweet lips
remember
aero-planes
remember
sugar
&
cream

move back
to the dark
their eyes
blind
to to
morrow

still
her
reflected light
in
their minds
breeds
picnics
fire
trucks
dogs
a river
a 1 cent kite
apples

petticoats
chamberpots
lemon peels
the fading
tickle
behind
the spine
when summer
time
lays petals
in the shade
where no
one
can
see

&

they finger
magazines

&

they wait
for the rest
of the
rush hr
dust
to sift in
to blanket
the last
of their days.

Culiacán

It's Christmas 1980
and a mourner has painted
"John Lennon
Don't Let Me Down"
on the fruit market wall.

Early morning,
a man sells oranges, and his belly
is stretched taut as a sack full of fruit.
Around him, boys thinner than his shadow
move pyramids of mango
like sugar
cannonballs.

Each second more is one second less.

Bloody goats grinning
chainsawed in half recline
on plywood counters.

Lolling tongues, valentine pink,
print hearts on skirts
of women.

Each second more is one second less.

Everywhere, bees.
Bees snipping off sugar
from dates. Bees licking up
caramel sweat.

67

Mountains
march all around the city,
connected at trunk and at tail.

     Each second more is one second less.

At the fishmonger's table
a mad boy in t-shirt
makes airplane sounds:
     Neeow
he says, and
     Zeeow!

Behind him, his father
feeds tuna to grinders,
albondigas flesh
curls out of their funnels.

The boy, as if hooked
to his father's machinery,
looks in our eyes
purses his lips
like a kiss
pushes out
one by one
like guitar picks
like snowflakes
the longest white scales
of a fish.

     Each second more,
     each second more.

Machetes

...meter tanto odio en las junturas de los besos.

—MANJARREZ

We drove a Mexican car
at speed through moonfields of beer—
Sinaloan hops, fat wheat heads, fire
weed. I was in love with
the driver's wife.

Lightning
bugs heated
to light and
burst.
Our windshield
streaky with glowing.

We drove out
the bottomland flats
to the coast. He confessed
he puked in her bed.
She raked the sheets free and washed them by hand.
The hands I prayed would touch me anywhere,
steeped in his alcohol stink.

I could do anything to him out there.
No one would know.
Then I could lie in her, lie to her,
give her back twenty years of all
I'd stored in my torso. Oh
I was a treasure chest of anger.

I wanted to strike myself inside her
like a match, light her petals,
feel her burn.
I wanted to feel
her eyelash
against my belly,
blink away
every hour
of night.

We spun off
the road, sat dumb
in blue dust, stumbled
out to piss together,
fools knee-deep in weeds,
flinging our lemon water. This
was my chance.
I turned
to start
the fight
when they
arose:

thin Indians
up from the fields
silent
sprouting men
ghost flowers
simply
there.

In each fist
a silver-bright machete.
Cold blades swept the air.
Moon slid oily down the blades, up
back down. A drop
of white light
like heavy fluid,
oblong on whetstone scratches.
Blades dripped moon.
And we both heard
the crackle within us
as insides creased
into paper.
The harsh sigh of our terror
followed us
as we ran
to the highway.

Since that night
we spend our nights
tearing those pages from our chests.
He is in his tropical house.
I am usually
in a hotel.
Sometimes I write her name
on mine, before I crumple them.
I write in the dark, eyes closed,
with invisible ink.
She turns back the blankets on another night,
his dead odors rising from her flesh.

I wipe rain drops on the sheets
of tissue that still bear her name.
Unspeakable poems for her.
Unknowable scents of her flowering.
I put my lips to her memory.

Then
        I light the flames.

Fall Rain

I paint myself in your sweat.
The blade of my hand peels
heat from your breasts.
Your heartbeat moves
my blood along the branches
of my wrists.

Under midnight's slate
can you tip this gray away?
Can you color my pale leaves
burn them red
before they fall, can you

lick this winter back
and rain

rain

rain your watersongs
across my lips
my hands

can you rain

inside my chest?

PART THREE

Father Returns from the Mountain

The Myth of Superman

I'm tired of writing

about my father

betraying

his skeleton

with confessions, allegations

bald

faced accusations. Yet,

one day crashes

through memory:

superhero cool.

One day

that makes his bones

stand tall in the afterland

his icy Mexico

of wondering souls he smokes

his cigarettes in now.

How

one day

driving

palm-treed National Avenue

in our bulbous World War Ford

down

toward Wabash

where the wrong side of town

our side of town

began:

green light down there

in the Wabash wash

big motor dragging us in

even Mom smoking,

Dad's square hand

clamped to the wheel.

How

a white woman

speeding from the 'hood never

saw the red light, never

saw us before her, never

even hit her brakes.

Slam!

Sudden storm of glass.

Ford high-side and flying.

Cutting blue-green steel arcs

through the air. And I,

in the back seat,

was suddenly

standing on the wind.

Drifting

weightless

out the shattered window.

Dad,

Superman,

held the wheel, reached

back,

his hand

coming for me

brushing Mom's hair

taking my collar

in his fist: Oh Superman

you took hold of me

and did not let go:

dragged me back

into life

guiding us through stunned cars

poles

scattering roadsigns:

you held me up,

just a fluttering

flag

made of your skin.

Raised.

Shaken.

Saved.

Father Returns
from the Mountain

The car is red. It has a sun-baked and
peeling black top. Little flakes of fake
leather blow away in the wind. The roof is
crushed. Windows are shattered. The front
end is crumpled. The axles are split and the
tires slant crookedly. Dry blood on the hood.
The steering wheel is twisted. Details of
violence. An American Motors Rambler 440,
1966 model. Slivers of glass are stuck in the
carpets. Dust settles on the stains. A
photograph of my father and me is caught under
the seat, fluttering like a flag, like a bird
trapped in the wind. There is a dime in the
broken driver's seat. Blood where the radio
should be. / This is the truth. The truth is
a diamond, or at least a broken mirror. There
are many reflective surfaces, and we observe
the ones we choose. We see what we can. / The
car is red. It stands in a dusty compound
among other crushed machines. A note to my
father in a flowery woman's hand blows out of
the glove compartment. It whispers "Querido
Alberto" a hundred times as it spins away.
There is a chain-link fence that rattles in a
breeze that smells of dogs and perfume. A
yellow sticker is pasted to the hood because

there is no glass to hold it. Children scare each other by touching the crusty patches of my father's blood. "He'll come back to eat you!" The dead man, the dead man. / A Mexican cop slides down the slope. He squints in the early morning sun. He can hardly see my father in the wreckage. He runs back up and calls for help. The blue light atop his car flashes, flashes, casting marching shadows over the rocks. Pink urine spreads across my father's clothing. The pain is a sound that hums inside his gut, that pierces his skull. Darkness. Sleep. / The telephone feels warm. I look out the window at a Monday sky. "Hello," he says. It is a family friend. "Do you remember me?" The morning sunlight reaches through the trees. "Of course I remember you. What's up?" His silence buzzes for a moment. When he speaks, he speaks carefully. "You father...has had an accident." "Is he hurt?" "Yes." "Badly?" "Yes." I lean forward. I think of my father being hurt. I think of him in pain. The tiny agony of tears pinches the corners of my eyes. / We are on a balcony in Puerto Vallarta. I am in love with the most inconceivable girl in Rosario, Sinaloa. Ebony crabs have come in from the jungle, mad with the rain that hasn't stopped for two days. They climb the stairs of the hotel, wait before our doors, attack us when we come out. His hand is on my shoulder.

I cannot contain the feelings as we watch
lightning bombard the hilltops. Rain
undermines the streets and floods the river
that eats great rifts in the jungle. We spend
the entire night in each other's confidence.
And when the tears come, he lets me cry. / My
father is severely damaged. His eyes are
open, but will not function. They scrape up
and down, but they cannot break the thick
shell of darkness that covers them. His body
will not move—he tells it to—to get the
hell up, get back in the car, light a
cigarette, go bowling, something. Anything.
But he is frozen. His mouth is a traitor that
will not function. It fills slowly with
liquid. When it reaches his lips, there is a
gradual, endless snail of red slipping down
his cheek and hiding in his ear. I am sitting
in my room listening to music. / "How bad?" I
ask, a little afraid, a little unwilling, a
little uncertain. "Very bad. He flew off a
mountain. He fell in the desert." The sun is
bright. / The car is red. The police
compound is quiet. A scrawny cat licks the
speedometer. / The police lift him into the
ambulance. He tries to talk he tries to see
he is a slab of meat and it makes him angry.
The pain makes him angry. The cuts on his
face sting. And through the morning, dawn
scorching the paper-sheet horizon, ravens
smelling the blood and exploding off the road

before them, the ambulance crew flies. To a
hospital—well, a clinic. Scorpions
drowsing in its shade. And there, the nurses
find him almost dead, and strip him bare, and
shoot a load of morphine in his fallen veins,
and tie him down in case he kicks, and leave
him naked eight hours alone. He knows he's
naked—God, he's mad. But the poppies
blooming in his arms send out their odors,
their perfume already bubbles up his throat,
and down, down, beyond his belly, to where the
memories dwell. The blood has made his throat
black. / I sit alone in the funeral home.
There is little sound from without: even
downtown Tijuana has to sleep. 3:00 a.m. No
sleep for me. Me and the body, we're wired. /
I open the coffin lid and look at him. He is
broken. His chin is a black openness. He was
always shaved pink and now little gray
whiskers are pushing their heads up through
the wounds. His shirt is stained. I put my
face to the side of the box and stare and
stare. I watch for a flicker, a twitch. I
wait for a microscopic flare of the nostrils.
The sealed eyelids seem ready to pop, to rise
and lower. I want, in terror, to see him lick
his lips so that I can break the Mexican
sealing glass, pull him up, save him, embrace
him. There is no movement. There is no
sound. / I found a photograph just yesterday.
In it, my father stands with the president,

with generals, senators. His captain's
uniform looks as crisp as a salad. At times,
I shuffle through his official papers and look
at his federal police badge. His smiles look
like mine. We are connected by the lips. The
grin is our chain. / I lie on the floor
beneath the coffin. He's up on a table laid
out like God's buffet. I close my eyes to
sleep, my last night beside him. I am a poet
at that instant. A shadow passes over my
face. I jump up, thinking that someone is
approaching. There is nothing. Again the
shadow. Again nothing. Again and again. I
imagine him waving farewell. As I slip into
sleep, I have a vision of a stiff hand
reaching for me over the edge. / The dreams
have come in a series. They are diamonds.
They are broken mirrors. In the first, I am
run over by a truck. My half-brother stands
on the curb and smiles down at me. I pull at
people's legs from the black street. / Death
is here now. I am finally aware of it.
Perhaps childhood is not knowing that it is
grinning at you from the corner. It has
pressed its face against the windows, it has
stalked in with the fog and awaits its turn. /
At 8:00 p.m. he tried to open his eyes. His
straining led to nothing. My father was born
in Rosario, little gem at the southern end of
Sinaloa. He died in San Luis Rio Colorado, a
dry husk in the north of Sonora. I can

imagine his gray hair against the pillow. His
lips, white, rolling back almost in a smile.
His abdomen searing red hot, then tingling pink
as he passed through to the new side.
Possibly music, a fragment of a tune wafting
through the haze. I hope he heard music. /
The family friend calls again. "Tell me," I
say. "His condition deteriorated for several
hours." "And?" "And your señor... rested."
"Dead?" "Dead." "Just now?" "Yes." "Thank
you." "Are you all right?" "Thank you." / No
one comes to the funeral home to spell me.
It's a wake, and I'm awake. I have watched
the corpse for seven hours. I have closed the
lid. I have not eaten since the day before.
"I hate waiting," I say out loud. His voice:
"I know, Son. I always hated it too. It's
boring." I spin around, but the lid remains
closed. There's nobody else in the room. "Do
you hear me?" I ask. "Yes," he replies. "I
love you," I say. "I know," he says. /
Mexicans love the dead. They are a lovely
treat with which to terrify each other.
Dawn's light, and people passing in the street
push open the door to peek at the coffin.
"What are you looking at, you vampires?" I
yell at them. "El muerto," they whisper. "El
muerto." / We carry the coffin to the
graveside. I have to go to the bathroom.
Dogs are running on the graves. Whores and
cops and ice cream men are working downtown.

People are eating and laughing and sweating and making love all over the world and my father is dead. The world has not even hesitated. Nobody has noticed. / The hard part is watching the box go down. Watching it being pushed into the black mouth, knowing that his flesh is being hid from you, and if you should search for a touch of it again you will find dusty corruption. The body goes. I walk away from the weeping. White clouds on the border. I keep my back to the mourners. Tijuana looks pretty from a distance. I was born there. / I sit in my house alone, working on the third draft of a book no-one will ever read. I hear a car in the driveway. When I open the door, the car is red. My dead father is leaning on the steering wheel. His hair is in disorder, his eyes are uncertain. I go to him, take his cold hand, lead him inside. He sits on the couch, settling like a white feather. "What happened?" he asks. I look into his face. *He doesn't know. He doesn't know he's dead.* Maybe I can fool him. Keep him alive. But I know as I hope it is impossible. I kneel at his feet. "Papá, you were killed." "Killed! But I'm right here!" "You were killed in an accident." "But the car's in the driveway. Brand new." "No." "It can't be," he says. I am afraid of hurting him, but I must. "Papá," I say, "go away. You're dead." "I can't be dead," he insists, pain and frustration mixing on his face. / As a child, I would ride standing beside him as he drove, holding tight to his shoulder. / I take his pant-legs in my hands. "Papá, go away. You can't stay here. You're dead!" He shakes his head sadly. I weep like his little boy wept, with my head on his knees. "You're dead, you're dead, you're dead." / A stonemason gets in the grave and spreads concrete over the box. We don't have enough money for a headstone. Maybe a tree will grow here, or a stand of mustard, goldenrod. Other mourners file in to feed the hole beside my father's. / The car is red. The cold desert wind moans in it at night. There is a scar on the mountain where he crashed. His glasses bend the moonlight between the crumbled rocks. / I hear his engine again. He looks much better. "Get in," he says. I get in. He takes me through miles and miles of dreamlands. Things that do and do not exist pass by, one after one. We are free to go anywhere we choose. He wants to go home to Rosario. / "Did it hurt to die?" I finally ask. "Well," he says, "it hurt before I died." "Were you afraid?" "Of course. I listened for you, but you never came." My stomach tightens. "I wanted to be there. I couldn't get to you. Don't you think it hurt me to let you die?" He smiles. "I know," he says. We pass the ruins of a railyard. "Your grandfather is proud of you," he says. I look at him. The tears come. I try to stop them, but they force their way out anyway. "I don't want to be without you," I blurt. He looks at me for a long while, then taps me on the knee. "You've got to stop crying. You sound like a little girl." Then: "You aren't without me. Remember that." His eyes are clear. "Where are your glasses?" I ask. "Back on the side of the road," he says. "But that's all right. I won't be needing them now." "Were you cognizant at the hospital?" I ask. "Yes," he says with disgust. "I was trapped inside that damned dead body. I hated that." "I'm sorry, Papá," I tell him. He looks at me. "Don't be sorry. You waste so much time that you need for yourself." I nod. "I closed the coffin," I say. "Thank you. I didn't want to be on display." I touch his arm. "Papá, did you... did you see God?" He smiles at me and turns on the radio. / When I was fourteen, my father and I spent hours laughing in the night about nothing, nothing at all. / The car is red. The driver's seat is torn. A beehive swells inside it. Bees fly where his eyes used to be. They fly through the air that used to touch his lips. They walk on the bent wheel that cracked his ribs. They sit where he used to sit. A slow, warm cascade of honey spreads over the traces of demolition. It is gold.

It catches the sunlight and reflect the clouds
that move in its depths, minute and sparkling
white. Droplets reflect the blue of the sky.
They hint at the smile in my father's eyes.

◆

Rosario, my earth

little town in which I learned to love

I dream of you, I miss you

thinking someday I'll return

Life took me from you,

but I never, never forgot you

my grandest illusion now

is to return to you once more

in the years of my nightfall

—Alberto Urrea
June 2, 1915 – January 10, 1977

APPENDIX

Translations of Spanish Text

(from page 25)

Ghost Sickness 14

My father, dead
now for interminable years, won't leave me
in peace: doesn't want to go: I see him
every day. My old man hides
in trees, in water, in
clouds of smoke escaping
from secretary's cigarettes. Or he enters
like a thief
through my windows
& he steals my food. He's a live-wire: he's capable
of hiding himself on the moon.
& he tells me,
>   —Son, nothing remains
>   Nothing remains.

My father, planted
in his Mexican soil, laying roots
into the dark meadow of forget, shines:
when I turn off the lamp, his face
throws sparks in the corner. When
I make love, he comes
running. When I step out
to the street, he pursues me
through the eyes
of homeless children.
He wears heels of gold.
He smells my coffee.
I see him
without seeing.
& he says,
>   —Son, nothing remains.
>   Nothing remains.

My father, dead already and turned to dust, cries
tears of clay. With the voice of stones he shouts, he sings
his final advice:

> —Son, your life is one coin.
> Spend yourself well. For
> nothing remains.
> Nothing remains of me.

(from page 34)

The Lost Face

It's winter
& I write to you
across this long silence.
If you could see what I've left
beneath the little black sky
of these plains. 1,000 figurines
of lead. My name.
Photographs
of a blue
dress. &
your face.

I am a sincere man
come from the deadlands of palm trees.
My infancy was
a garden of flame.
& you, what did you know
of me?
Before I touched your face
I watched you flee.

—Carmen

(from page 55)
From "Driving Away"

Sex. Labyrinth of shadows. *Aguardiente.* Red waves, veins, clouds. They made love: leaves fell, in the wind they galloped, the sound equal to the song of your nails scratching the floor. Foam. And there at your sides, you signed your name...blood on the wood. Sex. It's only a dream, and afterwards, you cannot remember the faces.

(from page 69)
From "Machetes"

...to insert so much hatred in the seams of kisses.
—MANJARREZ

LUIS ALBERTO URREA is the author of several books, among them *Across the Wire*. After doing relief work on the border for six years, he taught expository writing at Harvard. His fiction, non-fiction, and poetry are widely anthologized—most recently in *The Late Great Mexican Border* and in *The Best American Poetry*. He has received the Christopher Award, the Colorado Center for the Book Award, and the Western States Book Award for Poetry, among others. Currently, he is writer-in-residence at the University of Southwest Louisiana. He lives in Lafayette with his wife and new family.

Other Books by Luis Alberto Urrea
The Fever of Being (poetry; West End Press)
In Search of Snow (fiction; HarperCollins)
Across the Wire (non-fiction; Anchor)
By the Lake of the Sleeping Children (non-fiction; Anchor)

CINCO PUNTOS PRESS BOOKS
FROM THE BORDER & FROM MEXICO

Modelo Antiguo, A Novel of Mexico City, by Luis Eduardo Reyes,
(translated by Sharon Franco and Joe Hayes)

The Moon Will Forever Be a Distant Love, by Luis Humberto Crosthwaite,
(translated by Debbie Nathan and Willivaldo Delgadillo)

The Late Great Mexican Border, Reports from a Disappearing Line,
edited by Bobby Byrd and Susannah Mississippi Byrd

Women and Other Aliens, Essays from the U.S./Mexico Border, by Debbie Nathan

Dark and Perfect Angels, poems by Benjamin Alire Sáenz

Eagle-Visioned/Feathered Adobes, poems by Ricardo Sánchez

For more information or to receive a catalog, contact:

CINCO PUNTOS PRESS
2709 Louisville
El Paso, TX 79930
1-800-566-9072